WORLD IN
FOCUS

FOCUS ON
SOUTH AFRICA

JEN GREEN

WORLD ALMANAC® LIBRARY

Please visit our web site at: www.garethstevens.com
For a free color catalog describing World Almanac® Library's list of high-quality books
and multimedia programs, call 1-800-848-2928 (USA) or 1-800-387-3178 (Canada).
World Almanac® Library's fax: (414) 332-3567.

Library of Congress Cataloging-in-Publication Data

Green, Jen.
    Focus on South Africa / Jen Green.
        p. cm. — (World in focus)
    Includes bibliographical references and index.
    ISBN-13: 978-0-8368-6738-1 (lib. bdg.)
    ISBN-13: 978-0-8368-6745-9 (softcover)
    1. South Africa—Juvenile literature. I. Title.
    DT1719.G735   2007
    968—dc22   2006025095

This North American edition first published in 2007 by
World Almanac® Library
A Member of the WRC Media Family of Companies
330 West Olive Street, Suite 100
Milwaukee, WI 53212 USA

Commissioning editor: Nicola Edwards
Editor: Nicola Barber
Inside design: Chris Halls, www.mindseyedesign.co.uk
Cover design: Wayland
Series concept and project management by EASI-Educational Resourcing
(info@easi-er.co.uk)
Statistical research: Anna Bowden
Maps and graphs: Martin Darlison, Encompass Graphics

World Almanac® Library editor: Gini Holland
World Almanac® Library cover design: Scott Krall

Picture acknowledgements. The author and publisher would like to thank the following for allowing their pictures to be reproduced
in this publication:
CORBIS *cover top*, 4, 37, 45 (Gideon Mendel), 5 (Peter Turnley), 6 (Martin Harvey), 9 (Hulton-Deutsch Collection), 10, 11 (Bettmann), 13
(Reuters), 15 (Rob C. Nunnington; Gallo Images), 16 (Wayne Conradie/epa), 20 (Richard T. Nowitz), 21, 32 (Charles O'Rear), 28, 39,
41, 57 (Mike Hutchings/Reuters), 27 (Michael S. Lewis), 29 (Owen Franken), 30 (Caroline Penn), 34 (Wally McNamee), 38 (Jon Hicks),
46 (Anthony Bannister; Gallo Images), 49 (Ed Kashi), 51 (Mike Blake/Reuters), *cover bottom,* 53 (Louise Gubb), 56 (Sergio Pitamitz), 58
(David Lewis/Reuters); CORBIS Saba 12, 23, 31 (Louise Gubb); CORBIS Sygma 25 (Silva Joao), 36 (UN/DPI), 54 (Jon Hrusa/I); EASI-
Images *title page* 8, 14, 17, 19, 22, 24, 26 (Tony Binns), 18, 33, 35, 40, 42, 43, 44, 47, 48, 50, 52, 55, 59 (Roy Maconachie).

The directional arrow portrayed on the map on page 7 provides only an approximation of north.
The data used to produce the graphics and data panels in this title were the latest available at the time of production.

Printed in China

1 2 3 4 5 6 7 8 9 10 09 08 07 06

CONTENTS

Cover: A steam train crosses the bridge at Dolphin Point, near Wilderness, on South Africa's scenic southern Garden Route.

Title page: Table Mountain rises above Cape Town.

CHAPTER 1

South Africa – An Overview

The Republic of South Africa is Africa's wealthiest economy. Occupying less than one-twentieth of the continent, it produces about 40 percent of Africa's manufactured goods, nearly 50 percent of its minerals, and more than half its electricity. South Africa's economic success is founded on mineral wealth, including gold, diamonds, and coal. It also has the best-developed and maintained infrastructure, including transportation and communications, of any African nation.

RADICAL CHANGE

South Africa is a major force in both African and world politics. It is now among the most liberal democracies in Africa, with a constitution banning discrimination of any kind. Until the 1990s, however, South Africa was ruled by one of the world's most repressive regimes. It underwent radical and tumultuous change in the early 1990s. For more than a century, a small minority white population—of mainly Dutch or English descent—ruled this predominantly black nation. Whites owned most of the land and lived a comfortable lifestyle by exploiting South's Africa's mineral riches and its nonwhite population. The majority black population mainly lived in

▼ On April 27, 1994, long lines formed all over South Africa as people waited to vote in the country's first-ever democratic election.

poverty. They were not allowed to vote. Throughout the 1900s, nonwhite South Africans waged a tremendous struggle against white rule: first by peaceful means, such as demonstrations, and finally by civil disobedience and sabotage. In the 1950s, some of the white minority, known as Afrikaners, had introduced a system of racial separation to enforce their rule. The system was known as *apartheid*, which means "apartness" in Afrikaans, the Afrikaner language. In the 1960s and 1970s, the ruling National Party introduced increasingly repressive laws to maintain white control. South Africa became more and more isolated as countries around the world condemned its racist regime. As apartheid intensified, it looked as if the country was heading for bloody revolution. Instead, in about 1990, the National Party finally bowed to both internal and external pressures and began to dismantle apartheid. Within a few short years, the whole system was overturned in a "negotiated revolution." The African National Congress (ANC), which had opposed white supremacy since the early 1900s, swept to victory in the country's first democratic election in 1994. Nelson Mandela, jailed for twenty-seven years because of his opposition to apartheid, became the first democratically elected president.

In 1994, Mandela vowed to build a society in which "all South Africans, both black and white, will be able to walk tall, without any fear in their hearts." The new government faced enormous challenges. Radical political change did not provide an instant cure for the huge inequalities that had arisen under white rule. Since 1994, the government has done much to improve housing, general living standards, and educational and job opportunities for nonwhites. Deep divisions still exist, however, within South African society in terms of wealth, land, education, and

employment. About half the country's population still lived in poverty in the early 2000s. Meanwhile, new challenges arose, including HIV/AIDS on an epidemic scale.

▲ On February 11, 1990, Nelson Mandela addressed a huge crowd of antiapartheid supporters just hours after his release from prison.

LAND AND PEOPLE

Located at the southern tip of Africa, South Africa shares borders with Namibia, Botswana, Zimbabwe, Mozambique, and Swaziland. It completely encloses the land-locked country of Lesotho. Measuring up to about 870 miles (1,400 km) from north to south and 990 miles (1,600 km) from east to west, South Africa is about twice the size of Texas. It is a land of great natural beauty and scenic variety. Much of the country is a high plateau with rolling grasslands, but it also holds fertile valleys, craggy peaks, and large expanses of scrubland and desert. South Africa's scenic beauty, sweeping beaches, and spectacular wildlife create the basis of its thriving tourist industry. South Africa supports not one but three capitals. Pretoria (Tshwane) in the northeast is the administrative capital, home to many government buildings. Cape Town, in the southwest, is the legislative capital, the seat of parliament. Bloemfontein, in the center, is the judicial capital, location of the Supreme Court.

South Africa is one of the most ethnically diverse countries in Africa. As well as a majority black population made up of Zulu, Xhosa, and many other groups, the country also has the largest population of Europeans, Indians, and people of mixed race (also known as Coloureds) of any African nation. It is nicknamed the "rainbow nation" because of this diversity.

Reflecting its ethnic makeup, the country has eleven official languages: Afrikaans, English, and nine Bantu languages: isiNdebele, North Sotho, Setswana, Sesotho, siSwati, Shangaan-Xitsonga, isiVenda, isiXhosa and isiZulu. South Africa is second only to India in its total of official languages. Xhosa is known for its "click" syllables, with eighteen different click sounds. Zulu is the most widely spoken language in South Africa, but English is increasingly used to bridge language barriers. Some sections of the population are concerned that English is becoming more dominant at the expense of certain African languages. In addition to these official languages, many other languages and dialects are also spoken.

Physical Geography

- Land area: 471,008 square miles/ 1,219,912 square kilometers

- Water area: 0 sq miles/0 sq km

- Total area: 471,008 sq miles/ 1,219,912 sq km

- World rank (by area): 25

- Land boundaries: 3,021 miles/4,862 km

- Border countries: Botswana, Lesotho, Mozambique, Namibia, Swaziland, Zimbabwe

- Coastline: 1,739 miles/2,798 km

- Highest point: Njesuthi 11,181 feet/3,408 m

- Lowest point: Atlantic Ocean (0 feet /0 m)

Source: CIA World Factbook

◀ South Africa's beautiful scenery and spectacular wildlife are a major draw for tourists.

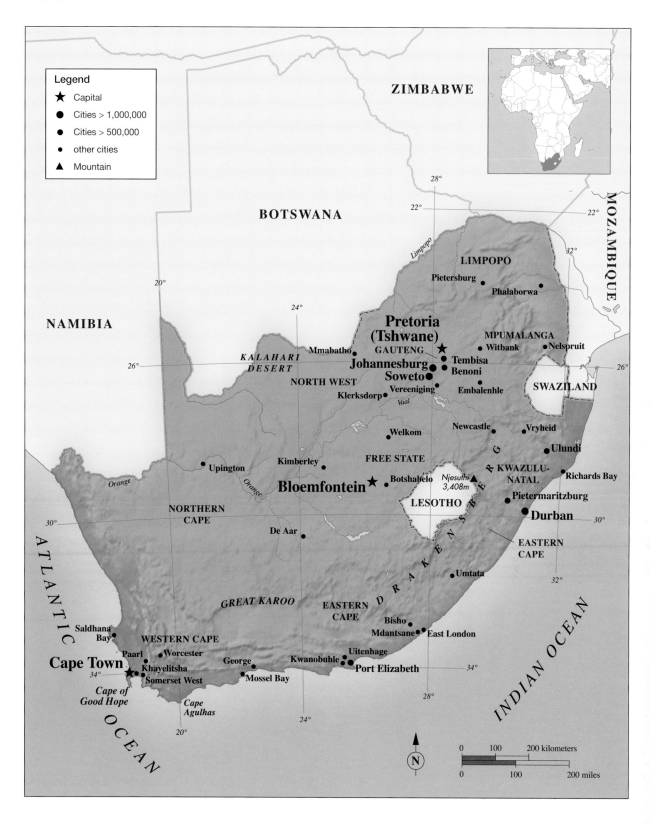

Legend
★ Capital
● Cities > 1,000,000
● Cities > 500,000
• other cities
▲ Mountain

ZIMBABWE

MOZAMBIQUE

BOTSWANA

28°

22°   22°

32°

LIMPOPO

Limpopo

Pietersburg

Phalaborwa

20°

NAMIBIA

24°

Pretoria
(Tshwane)

MPUMALANGA

*KALAHARI
DESERT*

GAUTENG

Mmabatho

Witbank

Nelspruit

26°   26°

Johannesburg

Tembisa

Soweto

Benoni

NORTH WEST

Vereeniging

Embalenhle

SWAZILAND

Klerksdorp

Vaal

Welkom

Newcastle

Vryheid

Ulundi

FREE STATE

KWAZULU-
NATAL

Kimberley

Orange

Upington

Bloemfontein

Botshabelo

*Njesuthi
3,408m* ▲

Richards Bay

Orange

Pietermaritzburg

NORTHERN
CAPE

LESOTHO

Durban

30°   30°

De Aar

EASTERN
CAPE

32°

Umtata

GREAT KAROO

EASTERN
CAPE

D R A K E N S B E R G

INDIAN OCEAN

Bisho

Mdantsane

East London

Saldhana
Bay

WESTERN CAPE

Uitenhage

Paarl

Worcester

George

Kwanobuhle

Cape Town

Khayelitsha

34°   Port Elizabeth   34°

Somerset West

Mossel Bay

28°

*Cape of
Good Hope*

*Cape
Agulhas*

24°

20°

A T L A N T I C   O C E A N

N

0   100   200 kilometers

0   100   200 miles

CHAPTER 2

History

The first inhabitants of South Africa were the San (Bushmen) and Khoekhoen people, who roamed South Africa as hunter-gatherers some 10,000 years ago. By 2,000 years ago, the Khoekhoen had become sheepherders and cattle herders living as far south as the Cape. A little later, Bantu-speaking Nguni people moved into the area from farther north. These included the ancestors of the Zulu, Xhosa, and other groups that make up much of the modern black population. These groups herded cattle, forged iron, and built small settlements. During the fourteenth and fifteenth centuries, more African peoples moved into the area, including Sotho, Tswana, Tsonga, and Venda. Skilled metal workers and farmers, they developed villages and towns.

EUROPEAN SETTLERS

European settlement of South Africa began in 1652, when a Dutch trading company called the Dutch East India Company built a fortified settlement where Cape Town stands today. This port was used to refuel ships sailing between Europe, India, and the Far East. During the late seventeenth and eighteenth centuries, white settlement of the Cape expanded as the Dutch seized the lands of the Khoekhoen and Xhosa. Dutch farmers called Boers set up farms mainly worked by slaves brought from Indonesia, Madagascar, and India. A steady stream of new settlers arrived from Europe, including Germans and French Protestants called Huguenots.

In 1806, the British seized Cape Colony from the Dutch during the Napoleonic wars. Beginning in the

◀ This monument in Pretoria honors the Great Trek of the 1830s through the 1850s, when thousands of Boers migrated from Cape Colony to avoid British domination of their culture.

1830s, the Boers, also known as Afrikaners, moved to other parts of South Africa to escape British rule. They moved to Natal, and then, when this too was seized by the British, farther north again, where they set up two republics called the Transvaal and the Orange Free State.

The nineteenth century was a time of conflict between Europeans and Africans and also among black peoples as the Zulu, Sotho, and Ndebele sought to expand their lands. In the 1860s, the discovery of gold and diamonds in the Boer republics brought new waves of white settlers. Boers and British fought for control of mineral-rich lands during the Boer Wars of 1880–1881 and 1899–1902. At the same time, both the Boers and the British continued to seize African lands, overwhelming black resistance with superior weapons. The last armed black resistance was brutally suppressed in 1906. Meanwhile, new laws and taxes forced many black Africans into paid employment for whites.

▼ Beginning in the 1870s, the British waged a series of wars against the Zulus, Xhosa, and other African peoples. This drawing shows British officers returning from a negotiation with the Zulu chief Cetshwayo during a truce in the 1879 Zulu War.

WHITE RULE AND APARTHEID

In 1902, the Second Boer War ended in victory for the British. Eight years later, the British and Boer territories were combined to form the Union of South Africa, in which black Africans had few rights. The 1913 Natives' Land Act legalized the land seizures of the nineteenth century, setting aside all but 13 percent of the country for whites, despite the fact that whites made up only a small minority of South Africa's population. The 1923 Native Urban Areas Act required blacks in towns to live in areas separate from whites. The African National Congress (ANC, originally the South African Native National Congress) was formed in 1912 to oppose the dawning era of white supremacy, but its eloquent appeals for justice were ignored.

After World War II, the Afrikaner extremist National Party took power in South Africa. It set out to enforce white minority rule through a system of racial segregation called apartheid. All South Africans were classified by race, with blacks and whites required to live in separate areas and separated in public places such as buses, trains, schools, doctors' waiting rooms, toilets, and beaches. In every case, black South Africans were given resources and facilities inferior to whites. In response, the ANC and allied groups called for nonviolent protest against apartheid.

UPRISING

In 1960, a group of unarmed demonstrators gathered to protest against the racist Pass Laws

▼ During the apartheid era, blacks and whites had to travel in separate train cars. These black Africans occupied a "Europeans Only" train car legally reserved for whites during a protest in 1952.

in Sharpeville, Transvaal. The police opened fire on the crowd, killing 69 people and wounding 186 more. The Sharpeville Massacre caused a wave of unrest among the black population. The government banned the ANC and allied organizations. Activists, including Nelson Mandela, went underground and launched an armed force, *Umkhonto we Sizwe* (MK), the "Spear of the Nation." MK began a bombing campaign against physical targets such as government buildings that symbolized white rule. In 1962, many activists were arrested, including Mandela, who was sentenced to life imprisonment. With its leaders imprisoned, the ANC went into exile to continue the fight.

 Did You Know?

In 1961, *Umkhonto we Sizwe* stated: "The time comes in the life of any nation when there remain only two choices: submit or fight. That time has now come to South Africa."

Focus on: The Pass Laws

The 1950 Population Registration Act classified South Africans into four racial groups: blacks, whites, Indians, and Coloureds. The classification affected every aspect of people's lives, including where they could live and work, their schooling, and their freedom of movement. The 1952 Pass Laws required nonwhites to carry an identity card or pass at all times. Blacks had to leave whites-only cities by sunset, except for maids working for white households, who were required to live in separate quarters. Anyone found without a pass could be arrested. In the 1950s, the ANC called for mass action against the Pass Laws. Many people burned their passes and 8,000 people were arrested.

▼ South African police inspect the bodies of the unarmed protestors they had shot dead during the Sharpeville Massacre in 1960.

LIFE UNDER APARTHEID

The Bantustan Acts of the 1960s and 1970s strengthened previous acts that had confined black Africans to reserved areas. The new acts required almost all blacks to live in one of ten *bantustans*, or homelands, or in townships on the edges of white cities and industrial areas where they serviced white businesses and homes. Making blacks citizens of the homelands meant that they could be denied citizenship rights in South Africa itself. The United Nations and many countries condemned the new laws as a major violation of human rights and began to impose trade sanctions on South Africa.

For generations, black Africans had deliberately been given inferior schooling. In 1976, a new law required them to receive half their lessons in Afrikaans, the language of the white rulers. Thousands of young people protested against this law. When police fired on a demonstration in the township of Soweto near Johannesburg, more than 600 people were killed, including many children. Outrage swept the townships. The international community condemned the massacre, and the ANC called for the townships to rise up and become "ungovernable."

APARTHEID CRUMBLES

During the 1980s, the South African government became ever more isolated. Supporters of antiapartheid launched strikes and demonstrations on a massive scale. In 1983, the National Party announced a state of

▼ In 1989, the South African police were still using force to suppress antiapartheid protests. Here, a police helicopter sprays sand to disperse black demonstrators on a "whites-only" beach.

emergency, with new powers to put down the growing unrest. More than 3,000 people died and 30,000 were arrested in the following three years as violence also grew between the ANC and its main rival group Inkatha, a powerful Zulu political party headed by Chief Mangosuthu Buthelezi. Meanwhile, trade sanctions were crippling the economy. In addition, South Africa suffered defeat in a series of unofficial wars waged against other African countries opposed to apartheid, notably Angola.

By 1989, the country truly had become "ungovernable," as the antiapartheid demonstrators had hoped, and the National Party realized it could no longer maintain white minority rule. A new leader, F.W. de Klerk, was elected president. Within a few months, his government announced plans to replace apartheid with a new multi-racial democracy. The ANC was unbanned, political prisoners including Mandela were released, and the apartheid laws repealed. Black leaders began talks with the government to organize the changeover to majority rule. In 1994, South Africa held its first democratic election. The ANC took power with Nelson Mandela as president. The world's first-ever "negotiated revolution" had taken place.

Focus on: Nelson Mandela

Nelson Mandela was born in 1918. Trained as a lawyer, he joined the ANC to campaign for black rights. When the government banned the ANC in 1960, Mandela went into hiding and helped found *Umkhonto we Sizwe*. He was soon arrested and tried, along with 155 others, and was sentenced to life imprisonment. During the twenty-seven years he spent in jail, Mandela's fame spread worldwide. He came to symbolize the struggle against apartheid. Released in 1990, he was elected president in 1994. Among other accomplishments, he helped to form the groundbreaking Truth and Reconciliation Commission to help heal the social wounds of apartheid. Mandela stepped down as president in 1999.

◄ In 1993, F.W. de Klerk and Nelson Mandela were jointly awarded the Nobel Peace Prize for their work in bringing about a peaceful end to apartheid.

CHAPTER 3

Landscape and Climate

Occupying 471,008 sq miles (1,219,912 sq km), South Africa is about the size of France and Spain combined. The Atlantic Ocean forms the country's western boundary, with the Indian Ocean to the east. The waters of the two oceans mingle at Cape Agulhas, at Africa's southernmost tip.

GEOGRAPHY AND TERRAIN

Four main types of terrain are found in South Africa: plateau land, mountains, coastal plains, and deserts. A high plateau called the Veld, Afrikaans for field, covers much of the interior and extends northeast towards Zimbabwe. The Highveld, standing at altitudes ranging from 3,900 to 5,900 feet (1,200 to 1,800 meters), oversees much of the central area. In the northwest, the Middleveld lies at about 3,900 feet (1,200 m), while in the northeast, the Transvaal Basin is mostly less than 3,280 feet (1,000 m). To the east and south, the Veld is rimmed by a semicircular mountain chain called the Great Escarpment, which includes

▼ The distinctive flat-topped Table Mountain rises alongside Cape Town.

the craggy peaks of the Drakensberg, Afrikaans for dragon's mountains. The Cape Mountains rise in the south. Flat-topped Table Mountain, often spread with what locals call a "table cloth" of clouds, edges Cape Town. Two dry plateaus, the Great and Little Karoo, stretch between the Cape and Drakensberg ranges.

Much of South Africa's coastline is bordered by a strip of lowland. The western strip is quite narrow, just 37 miles (60 km) wide, while the eastern strip is more extensive, measuring 50 to 150 miles (80 to 240 km) wide. The eastern strip rises steeply to the Great Escarpment. In the northwest, the barren Kalahari Desert stretches into Botswana, while the Namib Desert occupies the western strip.

South Africa has few major rivers because of its mainly dry climate. The longest river, the Orange, runs 1,300 miles (2,100 km) from Lesotho west to the Atlantic Ocean. Other notable rivers include the Vaal, a tributary of the Orange, which is 745 miles (1,200 km) long, and the Limpopo, flowing 1,100 miles (1,770 km) from near Johannesburg to the Indian Ocean in Mozambique. Agriculture, cities, and industry are steadily increasing water use and depleting South Africa's rivers and limited groundwater supplies.

Focus on: Natural Hazards

The most serious natural hazard in South Africa is drought. One of the worst droughts of recent years was in 1991 to 1992. Bushfires sometimes start in drought-stricken areas. Another serious hazard, tropical storms called cyclones, may sweep in from the Indian Ocean in humid weather, damaging settlements on the east coast. Tornadoes may strike either coastal or inland regions in summer. In 1993, a powerful tornado killed seven people in the east of the country in the towns of Glencoe and Utrecht.

▶ The Orange River has worn a deep gorge where it flows through an area of soft rock in the Augrabies Falls National Park.

CLIMATE

Located about midway between the equator and the Antarctic, South Africa has a broadly mild, sunny climate with many regional variations. Situated in the southern hemisphere, winter falls between June and August, with summer between December and February. The main influences on regional climates are latitude, height above sea level, prevailing winds, and distance from the oceans. Mountains and plateaus have cooler temperatures than coastal regions. The city of Johannesburg, which lies on a high ridge called the Witwatersrand, has January averages of 64 °F (18 °C) and July averages of 50 °F (10 °C). In the highest parts of the Highveld, winter temperatures drop below freezing at night.

▼ A farmer of the Northern Cape finds his stock dead of thirst during a drought in 2004. Six regions of South Africa were declared disaster zones during this drought, the worst in a century.

The southwest has a Mediterranean climate, with warm, dry summers and cool, wet winters. Cape Town has average January highs of 79 °F (26 °C) and midwinter lows of 45 °F (7 °C). In the east, the warm, southward-flowing ocean currents of Mozambique and Agulhas give the coastal strip a subtropical climate with hot, humid summers and dry, bright winters. The

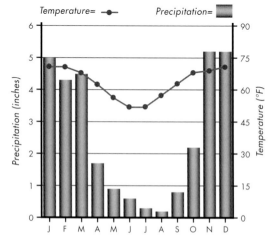

▲ Average monthly climate conditions in Pretoria

east coastal port of Durban has average January temperatures of 75 °F (24 °C) and winter averages of 64 °F (18 °C). The Benguela Current flows north along the West Coast, bringing cooler temperatures to the western coastal strip.

Rainfall is generally low and unreliable in South Africa, and droughts occur when the rains fail, which is often. Rainfall decreases from east to west, with the east and south being the wettest regions, while the north and west are much drier. The eastern strip is watered by moist winds blowing off the Indian Ocean with some places receiving 39 inches (100 centimeters) of rain yearly. The cold Benguela Current lowers temperatures along the West Coast, which prevents rain clouds from forming. Desert conditions, with less than 2 inches (5 cm) of rain yearly, prevail in parts of the north and west.

 Did You Know?

Sixty-five percent of South Africa receives less than 20 inches (50 cm) of rainfall a year.

VEGETATION

Climate, terrain, and soil type produce a huge range of vegetation in South Africa. The humid east coast supports subtropical vegetation including yellowwood and ironwood trees and coastal mangroves. The plateau land of the Veld is covered with savannah grasslands scattered with acacia trees, with the more densely wooded Bushveld in the northeast. In the west, dry Namaqualand bursts into a carpet of flowers after winter rains have fallen. The Southwestern Cape is famous for its unique vegetation, known as fynbos (Afrikaans for fine-leaved bush). Plants in the fynbos biome include colorful proteas, ericas, pelargoniums and irises.

Did You Know?

South Africa enjoys a huge variety of plants—more than 23,000 species and one-tenth of the world's plants. Many grow in a biome, the fynbos, that is found only in South Africa.

▼ The king protea, South Africa's national flower, is a great example of its unique fynbos vegetation.

CHAPTER 4

Population and Settlements

According to figures compiled in the census of 2001, South Africa's population is made up of 79 percent blacks, 9.6 percent whites, 8.9 percent people of mixed race, and 2.5 percent Asians. The black population consists of many different groups, each with its own cultural heritage, language, and traditions. The largest group, the Nguni, includes Zulu, Xhosa and Swazi. The next-largest, Sotho, includes Sesotho, Bapedi and Tswana. The Shangaan-Tsonga and Venda are also major groups.

Most whites are of European descent, of either Dutch, German, French-Huguenot, or British extraction. The term Coloureds, used for people of mixed race, includes the "Cape Malays," the descendants of Southeast Asians brought to Africa as slaves, and the Khoisan (the collective name for the Khoekhoen and San peoples), the original inhabitants of South Africa. The Asian population is mostly Indian, descended from indentured laborers brought to work in the plantations of Natal in the nineteenth century. Other substantial populations include more than 10,000 Chinese.

POPULATION GROWTH AND DENSITY

The number of whites who left South Africa either during or following the apartheid years affected population figures. In 2005, South Africa had a population of 47.4 million. The population grew rapidly from the 1970s to the 1990s. From 2000 to 2005, however, it grew by just 0.6 percent per year. South Africa's population is now forecast to fall slightly, to

 Did You Know?

Only a few San and Khoekhoen remain in South Africa. Small groups of San (Bushmen) live a nomadic life in the Kalahari Desert.

◀ South African society is now better integrated than at any time during the twentieth century. These medical students attend the University of Cape Town.

42 million by 2030. The major reason for the recent decline in population growth is the high number of people with HIV/AIDS, which has caused the overall mortality and infant mortality rates to rise since the 1990s. In 2003, a little less than one-third of the population was under 15, with nearly two-thirds aged between 15 and 64, and only a small fraction more than 65.

Although the average population density across the whole of South Africa is 100 per sq mile (39 people per sq km), in practice the population is unevenly distributed. Very few people live in the north and northwest, where the dry climate makes farming difficult or impossible, and where there are few natural resources. The southwestern tip around Cape Town and the

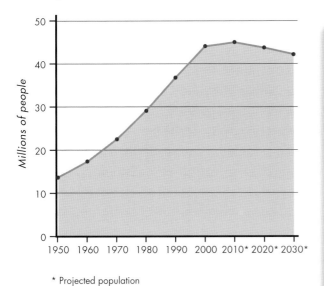

* Projected population

▲ Population growth 1950–2030

Population Data

- 🗁 Population: 47.4 million
- 🗁 Population 0–14 yrs: 32%
- 🗁 Population 15–64 yrs: 64%
- 🗁 Population 65+ yrs: 4%
- 🗁 Population growth rate: 0.5%
- 🗁 Population density: 100.6 per sq mile/ 38.9 per sq km
- 🗁 Urban population: 57%
- 🗁 Major cities: Cape Town 3,103,000 Johannesburg 3,288,000, Durban 2,643,000 Pretoria 1,282,000

Source: United Nations and World Bank

◀ A street market adds color to Johannesburg's high-rise city center. This former mining community is now the nation's largest city.

eastern coastal strip are both much more densely populated. On the Highveld, the Gauteng Province includes the large cities of Johannesburg, Soweto, Pretoria, and Vereeniging. The wetter climate of the south and east favors farming, while mining and industry also provide sources of employment.

URBAN AREAS

In 2003, 57 percent of the population lived in urban areas. This figure has risen steadily in recent decades. Cape Town, Johannesburg, and Durban are the largest cities, with more than 2.5 million inhabitants each. Other major urban

centers include Pietermaritzburg, Soweto, Pretoria, and Port Elizabeth.

During the twentieth century, racial segregation had a major impact on urban development. Sprawling black townships sprang up around whites-only cities to house the workers needed to run mines, factories, and service industries. Originally, the townships were makeshift shanty settlements. Permanent dwellings were built starting in the 1940s, but before 1994, most homes in townships lacked electricity or proper sanitation. Townships also had few facilities such as shops, parks, schools, or community centers. Starting in 1994, the government began a huge building and modernizing program, but progress has been slow. Many homes in townships are still without adequate sanitation and power supplies.

During the apartheid era, many township-dwellers traveled long distances each day to work in city centers. In the post-apartheid era, some black families have moved closer to city centers. In general, urban dwellings still reflect the gulf between blacks and whites. Leafy suburbs that were once legally declared whites-only districts have luxury homes with swimming pools. Most of these homes remain white-owned today, in spite of the end of legal segregation.

RURAL AREAS

About 43 percent of South Africa's population, predominantly blacks, live in rural areas. Here, too, facilities are often basic, with many homes lacking plumbing and electricity. Traditional dwellings are thatched with straw and often

◀ Most of the houses in the exclusive beach-front neighborhood of Clifton in Cape Town are still owned by whites.

Focus on: Building New Homes

In 1994, the new government inherited the housing crisis of the apartheid era, with up to 3 million families homeless and up to 8 million people living in shanty towns or squatter camps. Its Reconstruction and Development Programme (RDP) included a major building program, with the challenge of constructing 300,000 new homes before 2004. New suburbs now cover large areas on the outskirts of cities. Shortage of housing, however, is still a major problem in cities because, despite the government's efforts, the demand for housing in cities has outstripped the provision of new housing. This housing demand is largely a result of mass migration into the cities from rural areas. In 2003 through 2004, an estimated 7 million people were still living in shanty towns.

built of mud bricks. Zulu and Xhosa homes are traditionally circular, while traditional Ndebele and Basotho homes are rectangular and painted with brightly colored geometric designs.

The land acts of the twentieth century uprooted millions of black Africans from their homes. The white government forcibly moved blacks to poor, dry areas that became the bantustans (homelands). Small-scale black farmers were turned off their lands. During these forced relocations, thousands of people were simply abandoned without housing or employment. During the apartheid era, bantustan populations consisted largely of women, children, and older people. To support their families, men worked as migrant laborers in distant mines and factories. Since 1994, the new government has been challenged to right some apartheid injustices, including restoring confiscated lands.

▼ Ndebele women traditionally hand paint the walls of their homes in bold patterns and colors.

CHAPTER 5

Government and Politics

South Africa has been a republic since 1961, when it was expelled from the British Commonwealth. It is a parliamentary democracy with a constitution dating from 1996. Since 1994, everyone over the age of eighteen has had the right to vote. Before that time, black Africans, the majority, had no vote.

NATIONAL AND REGIONAL GOVERNMENT

South Africa's parliament is made up of two houses. The upper house, the National Council of Provinces, has 90 members, with 10 members elected from each province. The lower house, the National Assembly, has 400 members, with half being drawn from national and half from provincial lists. Members are elected by proportional representation, and elections are held every five years. The president is head of government, and appoints the Cabinet. Unlike many other nations, he or she is also head of state. Thabo Mbeki of the ANC has been president since 1999, when Nelson Mandela stepped down.

The Republic of South Africa incorporates all the former bantustans. It is divided into nine provinces: Limpopo, North West Province,

▼ The South African government is based at parliament buildings in the legislative capital, Cape Town.

Gauteng, Mpumalanga, KwaZulu-Natal, Free State, and the Northern, Western, and Eastern Capes. Provincial governments are headed by an elected premier, who appoints an executive council. Both provincial and local councils have considerable independence on issues such as taxation. In addition, a council of traditional leaders advises the government at the national, provincial, and local level.

CONTEMPORARY POLITICS

Since 1994, the African National Congress (ANC) has been the most popular party in South Africa, winning 69.7 percent of the vote in the 2004 election. It currently rules in coalition with the Inkatha Freedom Party (IFP), led by Chief Mangosuthu Buthelezi. Other important political parties include the Democratic Alliance (DA), the African Christian Democratic Party (ACDP), the Pan-Africanist Congress (PAC), and the United Democratic Movement (UDM). In addition, both the Communist Party and the Congress of South African Trade Unions (COSATU), active

in the antiapartheid movement, are formally allied with the ANC. Some sections of the population, notably Zulu speakers in KwaZulu-Natal, want more autonomy and even independence for certain regions.

Focus on: The Bill of Rights

South Africa's Bill of Rights (which forms part of the 1996 constitution) is among the most liberal and comprehensive in the world. It outlaws discrimination on the grounds of race, religion, gender, language, and sexual orientation. All citizens are equal before the law and guaranteed freedom of opinion, belief, and, critically, the newly-won freedom of movement.

 Did You Know?

The National Party (the all-white, ruling party of the apartheid era) disbanded in 2005 after failing to win a significant share of the vote in several elections.

◀ Presidential candidate, now president, Thabo Mbeki of the ANC campaigns before the 1999 election. The ANC, the party that led all others in the antiapartheid fight, has dominated elections since 1994.

RIGHTING WRONGS

In 1994, the newly-elected government faced immense challenges. The ANC's landslide victory did nothing to change the fact that much of the country's land, wealth, and business lay in the hands of whites. Most blacks, Coloureds, and Asians were less well-educated, with inferior housing and medical services and higher unemployment. The new government's task amounted to a comprehensive reorganization of society aimed at a fairer distribution of resources. Part of its response was to launch the ambitious Reconstruction and Development Programme (RDP), a 25-year plan to redistribute land, provide jobs, and improve housing, medical care, and education.

Part of the funding for the RDP came from raising taxes and making cuts in government spending, but much came from private business and foreign aid. By 2004, South Africa had built up foreign debts estimated at $27 billion.

Since 1994, the government has made great strides in raising living standards for blacks, Coloureds, and Asians, but inevitably there are many who feel that progress has been slow. At the other end of the scale, some whites feel that ANC policies have made it difficult for them to find work. Under apartheid, high-paying jobs were reserved strictly for whites. Now whites

▼ Construction workers labor on a building site in Welkom, Free State, in the mid-1990s. This project was one of the many undertaken as part of the Reconstruction and Development Programme of the post-apartheid years.

must compete with everyone else for the first time. The government's Black Economic Empowerment programme (BEE) has proved controversial in its moves to correct racial imbalance in the management of industry and business, where white managers continue to dominate.

As well as the social challenges outlined above, the government also faces a major problem with HIV/AIDS and a very high rate of violent crime, including murder, rape, assault, and theft. During apartheid and in the campaign for the 1994 elections, many acts of violence were committed by all sides, including the white security forces, the ANC, and Inkatha, all vying for power. The Truth and Reconciliation Commission did much to reduce racial tensions, but many criticize the government's record on law and order, condemning both the police and courts as inept. Since 1994, there have been allegations of corruption within the police force, legal system, and even government ministries. In June 2005, vice president Jacob Zuma was forced to resign after his financial advisor was accused of corruption.

Focus on: The Truth and Reconciliation Commission

◀ No one was exempt from appearing before the Truth and Reconciliation Commission. Winnie Madikizela-Mandela, former wife of Nelson Mandela, appeared before the commission in 1997 to answer allegations of wrongdoing, such as supporting violence in the last days of apartheid.

The South African government's ground-breaking Truth and Reconciliation Commission was set up in 1995 to heal the wounds of apartheid. Chaired by Archbishop Desmond Tutu, it investigated human rights violations committed between 1960 and 1994. The televised sessions heard statements from thousands of victims and also self-confessed apartheid criminals. It awarded compensation and gave amnesty to those whose crimes were "politically motivated." The Commission found the minority white government and also both the ANC and Inkatha guilty of violent acts.

CHAPTER 6

Energy and Resources

South Africa's rich mineral resources include gold, diamonds, and abundant coal for energy. Natural resources include good farmland, fish in the surrounding seas, and also tremendous scenic beauty and wildlife, which strongly encourage the tourist industry.

ENERGY RESOURCES AND USE

South Africa's energy sector is well developed. It is the African continent's leading energy producer—and consumer. Coal is its main source of energy. The country has huge reserves of this fossil fuel—enough to meet its own energy needs and also to make it the world's third-largest coal exporter in the early 2000s. The nation's sixty coal mines provide the raw materials for more than 90 percent of its electricity production. South Africa also has reserves of natural gas but no oil. A South African company called Sasol converts coal and gas into synthetic gas and diesel that are used as fuels. Hydroelectricity is well developed. Dams and hydroelectric plants on the Orange River provide energy and also water for agriculture and nearby cities. Nuclear power contributed 5.4 percent of the nation's electricity in 2002.

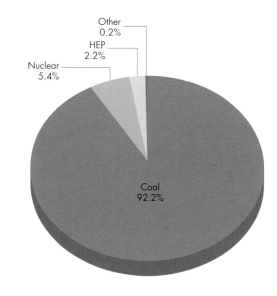

Other 0.2%
HEP 2.2%
Nuclear 5.4%
Coal 92.2%

▲ Electricity production by type

► A hydroelectric dam captures energy from the Orange River in the Free State. Hydroelectricity provides more than 2 percent of South Africa's electricity.

In 2005, South Africa ranked 26 in the world in terms of population, yet it used only slightly more than 1 percent of the world's energy. In that year, 46 percent of all energy used in South Africa was consumed by industry and nearly one-quarter by transportation, while domestic use accounted for more than one-fifth. In 1994, about half of the population was without electricity. Part of the 1994 election pledge was to supply electricity to millions of new homes by 2010. Large amounts of money are also being spent on updating the country's dilapidated electricity distribution network, particularly in rural areas.

Energy Data

- Energy consumption as % of world total: 1.1%
- Energy consumption by sector (% of total),

Industry:	46.2%
Transportation:	24.4%
Agriculture:	3.1%
Services:	3.7%
Residential:	20.9%
Other:	1.7%

- CO_2 emissions as % of world total: 1.5%
- CO_2 emissions per capita in tons per year: 7.3

Source: World Resources Institute

MINERAL WEALTH

South Africa's abundant minerals are a major source of income. The discovery of gold and diamonds in the 1860s, 1870s, and 1880s led to its transformation into an industrial nation. The world's top producer of gold, platinum, and chromium, South Africa also has rich reserves of manganese, nickel, copper, phosphates, uranium, silver, and iron ore.

From the late nineteenth century, gold and diamonds made vast fortunes for white mine-owners such as Cecil Rhodes of De Beers Consolidated Mines. Meanwhile, thousands of black miners endured harsh and extremely dangerous conditions for very little pay. During the early twentieth century, black and migrant workers were treated little better than slaves, being housed in racially-segregated compounds even before apartheid. Since 1994, the government and mining unions have worked together to improve conditions in the mines.

 Did You Know?

In 1905, the world's largest diamond was found near Pretoria. It was cut to form 105 stones, of which the biggest, the Star of Africa, now forms part of the British crown jewels.

◀ A miner works deep underground at a gold mine in Carletonville. Despite modern technology, gold mining is still a dirty and sometimes dangerous occupation.

Focus on: Gold and Diamond Mining

South Africa's main gold-bearing rocks lie in the Witwatersrand, a 267-mile (430-km) arc between Free State and Mpumalanga. In 1886, a poor prospector named George Harrison discovered gold at what is now Johannesburg. His discovery sparked one of the biggest gold rushes in history. In just three years, the mining town that sprang up became South Africa's largest city. Originally, gold was found at the surface, but now most gold-bearing rocks lie deep underground. Diamonds were first discovered in South Africa in 1867. Four years later, a rich diamond field was located at Kimberley. The site is now the location of the world's deepest artificial hole.

▲ A South African fisherman tosses his catch ashore at a Cape Town harbor. In 2005, South Africa took part in a major summit on the fishing industry's role in reducing poverty in Africa.

FISHING, FORESTRY, AND FARMING

With about 1,740 miles (2,800 km) of coastline, South Africa's fishing industry is important. The waters off the west coast are the main fishing grounds. Here the upwelling of cold, mineral-rich water nourishes the microscopic plankton that provide food for an abundant and diverse supply of fish. Hake, anchovies, pilchards, mackerel, and herring are all commercially important. Fishing is regulated by the government to preserve fish and shellfish stocks.

Only 4 percent of South Africa is forested. In the nineteenth century, large tracts of yellowwood and ironwood trees were felled, reducing the nation's already scant timber stocks. Currently, however, South Africa fulfills most of its own needs for timber and pulp through managed forestry and replanting.

Croplands occupy about 38 percent of South Africa, but only about 1 percent is under permanent cultivation. Irrigation is necessary in many areas. The main crop-growing regions are the south, east, and parts of the Veld. Major crops include maize, wheat, sugar cane, potatoes, and fruits such as apples, oranges, pineapples, bananas, and also grapes for wine-making. The main grape-growing area is the southern tip of the Western Cape. South Africa ranked among the world's top ten wine-producing nations in

▼ Workers harvest grapes at a vineyard in the Western Cape. This region is the center of the South African wine industry.

the early 2000s. Beef and dairy cattle are pastured on less fertile land, while sheep and goats graze on the dry terrain in the north and west and on the steep slopes of the Drakensberg.

Two main types of farming are practiced in South Africa: commercial and subsistence farming. Commercial farms are large-scale enterprises that use modern methods and employ mostly black labor. These traditionally white-owned businesses produce food for cities and also for sale abroad. Small-scale subsistence farmers, mainly black South Africans, grow food for their families using basic tools such as hoes. Any surplus food they produce is sold at local markets. From colonial times, many Africans were forced off their lands that were then converted to commercial farms and plantations. Since 1994, the government has worked to restore lands to evicted black farmers and to improve resources for subsistence farmers.

CHAPTER 7

Economy and Income

South Africa is Africa's most industrialized nation, producing up to 30 percent of the continent's entire Gross Domestic Product (GDP). Economic growth is supported by the country's well-developed infrastructure, which allows products to be efficiently transported both within South Africa and to neighboring countries. In 2003, it achieved economic growth of only 0.8 percent, but experts have predicted a period of strong growth for the coming years.

Did You Know?

In 2004, 30 percent of South African workers were employed in agriculture.

SOUTH AFRICA'S ECONOMY

Before the arrival of Europeans, most South Africans lived as herders and farmers, forming self-sufficient communities. Beginning in the seventeenth century, their traditional economy was disrupted, first by wars waged by whites

Focus on: Women Workers

South Africa has traditionally been a male-dominated society. During the nineteenth and twentieth centuries, women of all races generally received a less thorough education than men, with illiteracy high among many black women. Even in the late twentieth century, women were often paid less than men for the same work, and suffered discrimination that kept them from taking senior positions. In 1994, the ANC vowed to build a non-sexist society, working to correct the gender imbalance and fight discrimination in all sectors of employment.

◀ Women workers sew at a clothing factory in Soweto. In the textile sector, such factories are traditionally staffed by women who work for low pay.

▶ Impossible under apartheid, white and black stockbrokers now work side by side in a brokerage in Johannesburg. The city is a leading center for banking and finance.

and then by the introduction of new laws and taxes. The Hut Tax of the late nineteenth century required black Africans to pay the government a tax on their homes. Taxes forced many to work for money for the first time. Men left their villages to seek work in distant mines and factories—the start of the migrant labor system that caused so much hardship for black Africans. They had to leave their farms untended, causing widespread poverty.

The discovery of gold and diamonds in the late nineteenth century kick-started industrial development, which continued in the early twentieth century. The economy boomed in the 1950s and 1960s, but it was hit in the 1970s and 1980s by international sanctions that opposed apartheid. Ending apartheid ended the sanctions and helped the economy and tourism boom.

SERVICE INDUSTRIES

Service industries are the most important sector of the South African economy, employing 45 percent of the workforce and producing 65 percent of GDP in 2004. This sector includes finance, banking, tourism, transportation, education, government, and social services. Financial and legal services are strong, and tourism is a major source of foreign income.

Economic Data

▢ Gross National Income (GNI) in U.S. $:
165,326,000,000
▢ World rank by GNI: 30
▢ GNI per capita in U.S. $: 3,630
▢ World rank by GNI per capita: 94
▢ Economic growth: 0.8%

Source: World Bank

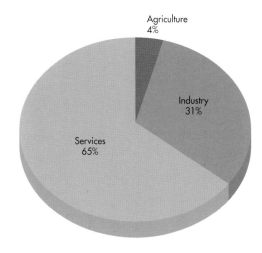

▲ Contribution by sector to national income.

ECONOMIC MAINSTAYS

Mining and manufacturing are mainstays of the South African economy. In 2004, 25 percent of the workforce was engaged in this sector, which yielded 31 percent of GDP. Many manufacturing industries were originally spin-offs from mining. For example, the iron and steel industry grew up to supply mining equipment, while vehicle manufacturing developed to aid the transportation of minerals. South Africa is the African continent's main manufacturing nation, and South Africa's most important products include vehicles —which contributed 6.4 percent to GDP in 2003—machinery and electronic equipment, iron and steel, cement, chemicals, fertilizers, textiles, processed foods, gems, and jewelry. Johannesburg, Durban, East London, and Port Elizabeth are major centers for industry and manufacturing.

WORKFORCE

In 2004, South Africa's workforce was estimated at 16.6 million, with about 26 percent of the working population estimated to be unemployed. This unemployment figure includes people working within the informal economy, doing mostly unskilled jobs such as work in the building trade, gardening, or selling goods on the streets, without being officially registered or paying tax. The government is currently trying to bring more informal-sector workers within the formal economy. Unemployment is particularly high among the black population because of the lack of training opportunities under apartheid. The Reconstruction and Development Programme and other government initiatives have been major sources of employment since 1994.

◀ A worker uses a precision tool to cut a diamond in Jewel City in Johannesburg.

In 2000, the ANC announced plans to foster economic growth and control inflation by increasing privatization, reducing government spending, and relaxing labor legislation. These moves, particularly the last, brought the government into conflict with trade union organizations such as COSATU, a traditional ally of the ANC. South Africa's economy is buoyed by foreign investment, which has risen steeply since 1994. The economy is still suffering from the legacy of apartheid, which fostered widespread poverty and a largely unskilled black workforce. Since 1994, the government has taken steps to tackle these obstacles to economic growth, but they remain daunting problems.

Focus on: A Divided Workforce

From colonial times through the apartheid era, South Africa's workforce was divided along racial lines. Whites received much better education, training, and job opportunities. As a result, they secured almost all of the skilled, technical, and managerial posts. Nonwhites were deliberately less well-educated. They did predominantly manual work and were prevented both by racism and by actual laws from pursuing many professional careers. Since 1994, the government has worked to tackle this imbalance through the Black Economic Empowerment Programme and other initiatives, but training takes time. A great shortage of skilled black workers continues.

▼ Unemployed women wait at an employment office in Cape Town. As South Africa recovers from apartheid, unemployment is still higher among blacks than whites.

CHAPTER 8

Global Connections

South Africa's ties with other nations include political, economic, and cultural connections. Cultural ties have been forged partly through human migration to and from South Africa since colonial times. From the mid-seventeenth century, European settlers began to arrive in increasing numbers. Slavery and the indentured labor system brought the arrival of other immigrants, including slaves from Southeast Asia and eastern and central Africa and indentured workers from India. Today, people of European, Indian, or mixed descent together make up about one-fifth of South Africa's population.

▼ A 1980s antiapartheid demonstration in Washington, D.C., demanded the U.S. government stop trading with South Africa. Such demonstrations took place in many countries around the world.

INTERNATIONAL RELATIONS DURING APARTHEID

South's Africa's political and economic links with other nations were severely damaged by apartheid. On gaining independence from Britain in 1910, South Africa became part of the British Commonwealth, but it was expelled in the early 1960s because of its severe human rights abuses and racism. Events such as Sharpeville also led to South Africa's expulsion from the Organization of African Unity (OAU, now African Union, AU) and from the United Nations (UN) in 1974.

As apartheid intensified, so the country became increasingly isolated. For example, many severe restrictions were imposed on international journalists reporting from South Africa. Foreign news and media within the country

▲ Tourists walk through the redeveloped Victoria and Alfred Waterfront in Cape Town. Tourism has boomed in South Africa in the post-apartheid years.

were strongly censored. Opposing apartheid, most countries cut their sporting ties with South Africa and cancelled international events.

During the 1970s and 1980s, criticism of apartheid grew internationally. Nelson Mandela became the world's most famous political prisoner, and campaigners in many nations demanded his release. A groundswell of public opinion called for foreign investors to withdraw their backing from South African businesses and for governments to impose trade sanctions. In 1986, the United States, the European Economic Community (EEC), and the British Commonwealth all imposed trade boycotts on South Africa in response to citizen pressure. The economic boom of the 1950s and 1960s had been largely fuelled by foreign investment, so the boycotts damaged South Africa. Trade sanctions undoubtedly played a part in forcing the National Party to open negotiations with

antiapartheid groups in 1990. In 1990, Nelson Mandela's release from prison was televised worldwide and watched by millions of people. In 1993, Mandela himself appeared at the UN, to request that trade sanctions on South Africa be lifted because the movement toward full, multiracial democracy had become unstoppable. Boycotts were duly lifted, and imports and exports began flowing again. Mandela's inauguration as president of the new, multiracial democratic South Africa was witnessed by the largest-ever gathering of international leaders. Sporting links were restored, and tourism quickly became a growth industry. The largely peaceful transition to full democracy was a source of great inspiration to human rights campaigners around the world.

POST-APARTHEID SOUTH AFRICA

In 1994, South Africa was welcomed back to the Organization of African Unity. Since democratization, South Africa has been involved in a number of peace talks between African nations, for example, in Ivory Coast, Burundi, and the Democratic Republic of the Congo. Not all aspects of South Africa's foreign policy are popular at home. The government has been widely criticized for its support of the repressive regime in neighboring Zimbabwe, led by Robert Mugabe. Mugabe overthrew the white-controlled regime of former Rhodesia but became a dictator who rigged elections.

CURRENT TRADE LINKS AND PARTNERS

South Africa's trading links have blossomed in the post-apartheid era. In 2004, the total value of the country's exports was U.S. $41.9 billion. Its main trading partners were the United States (10.2 percent of exports), the UK (9.2 percent), Japan (9.2 percent), Germany (7.1 percent), and the Netherlands (4 percent).

Did You Know?

South Africa receives millions of dollars in foreign aid each year: In 2000, the figure was U.S. $487.5 million.

Focus on: Border Disputes

Not all of South Africa's relations with its neighbors are peaceful. It has long-standing border disputes with both Swaziland and Namibia. The dispute with Swaziland dates back to the early 1900s, when Swaziland came under British rule. Some areas where Swazi people live have since become part of South Africa, and Swaziland would like the return of these areas.

South Africa's dispute with Namibia is about the exact location of the border between the two countries, and South Africa has troops positioned on the Orange River along this boundary. It also has troops along its border with Zimbabwe, to stem the flow of refugees from that country who are seeking work or fleeing Mugabe's repressive rule or actual political persecution.

◀ Nelson Mandela meets with Kofi Annan, secretary-general of the United Nations, during an Organization of African Unity (now the African Union) summit in 1997.

South Africa's chief exports include gold, diamonds, platinum, and other metals and minerals, as well as coal, machinery, weapons, and also foods.

In 2004, South Africa imported goods worth a total of U.S. $39.4 billion. South Africa's main imports are machinery and equipment, chemicals, petroleum products, scientific instruments, and foods. South Africa now plays an active role in many political and trade organizations, including the World Trade Organization, which promotes trade between member states, and the African, Caribbean, and Pacific Group of States (ACP). Links with other African nations are also increasing through the South African Development Community (SADC), which coordinates strategies for sustainable development in the region in areas such as trade and industry, food and agriculture, and infrastructure.

▶ Peaches are among the soft fruits grown for South African export market. During the apartheid era, South African export sales were badly hit by ongoing international trade boycotts.

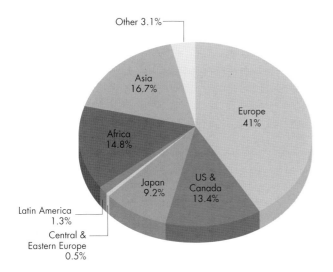

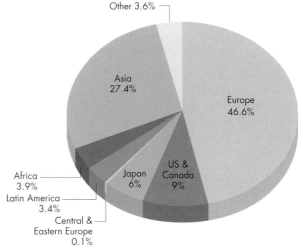

▲ Destination of exports by major trading region

▲ Origin of imports by major trading region

CHAPTER 9

Transportation and Communications

South Africa's transportation network is well developed. Ranked as the most efficient in Africa, it is also used by neighbors such as Namibia, Lesotho, and Mozambique. The transportation sector is a major employer.

RAIL AND ROAD

South Africa's extensive rail network was developed in colonial times to exploit the country's minerals. In 2004, it consisted of some 12,970 miles (20,872 km) of track, of which

Focus on: Gandhi and South African Railways

The Indian leader Mahatma Gandhi spent more than twenty years in South Africa (from 1893 to 1914) working as a lawyer. Although this was well before the apartheid era, discrimination by race was part of everyday life in South Africa. Gandhi's experience of racism on South African trains and elsewhere was important to the development of his ideas on nonviolent protest. For example, in 1893, Gandhi was ordered to leave a first-class train compartment, despite having a valid first-class ticket, because only whites could use first class. His nonviolent protest resulted in his being thrown off the train. After spending years opposing racism in South Africa, Gandhi returned to India, where his technique of passive resistance helped to free the country from British rule. Gandhi's nonviolent strategy also inspired U.S. civil rights leader Dr. Martin Luther King.

▼ A steam train crosses the bridge at Dolphin Point, near Wilderness, on the scenic southern Garden Route.

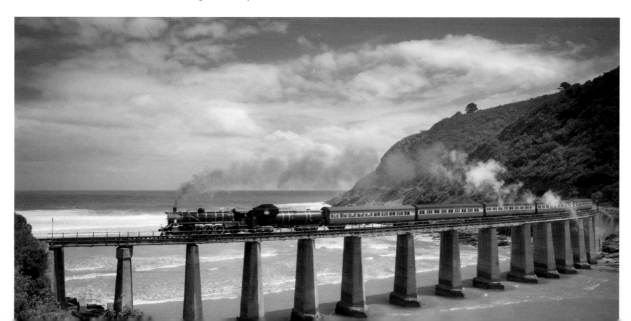

roughly half were electrified. Diesel and electric trains carry freight and millions of commuters daily, and old-fashioned steam trains are popular with tourists. During the apartheid era, there were separate train cars for whites and nonwhites. Dealing with segregation on South African trains helped the Indian politician Mahatma Gandhi create his nonviolent techniques to oppose British rule in India.

In the early 2000s, South Africa had 171,485 miles (275,971 km) of roads, of which less than one-fifth were paved. The country's roads were previously paved in places where they served white-owned businesses, while roads in rural areas were largely left unpaved. Expressways, however, link all major towns and cities, and huge amounts of freight go by road. In 2002, fewer than one in ten South Africans owned a car. Most people use public transportation, including buses, to go to work and for other trips. Three main kinds of buses serve the public: air-conditioned coaches for luxury travel, ramshackle "African buses," and cheap minibus taxis, many of which operate illegally.

 Did You Know?

During the apartheid years, in response to pressure from U.S. citizens against apartheid, the United States banned South Africa's national airline from using its airports.

Transport & Communications Data

- Total roads: 171,485 miles/275,971 km
- Total paved roads: 35,772 miles/57,568 km
- Total unpaved roads: 135,713 miles/218,403 km
- Total railways: 12,970 miles/20,872 km
- Airports: 728
- Cars per 1,000 people: 94
- Cellular phones per 1,000 people: 364
- Personal computers per 1,000 people: 73
- Internet users per 1,000 people: 68

Source: World Bank and CIA World Factbook

◀ Passengers stream through a minibus station in Cape Town. Minibuses provide a cheap form of transportation and are particularly popular among township dwellers.

AIR AND SEA

South Africa has three international airports: Johannesburg, Cape Town, and Durban. Daily flights link these major hubs with domestic airports at Pretoria, East London, George, Bloemfontein, Kimberley, and Port Elizabeth, which in turn are connected to smaller airports. Air travel is an important part of South Africa's infrastructure—for those who can afford it. South Africa's sea ports are among the busiest in Africa. The main ports are Cape Town, Durban, East London, Mossel Bay, Port Elizabeth, Richards Bay, and Saldhana. Shallows prevent large vessels from navigating the country's rivers.

PUBLIC TRANSPORTATION

During apartheid, the Pass Laws required all nonwhites to leave the cities where they worked at sunset and return to their townships or suburbs. This strained public transportation— and also people's pockets, because commuting

was expensive. It was also time consuming and crowded. Millions still must make long daily journeys from the townships to city centers. Public transportation remains overcrowded, costly, and sometimes dangerous because of the risk of mugging. The government has pledged action to ease these problems. New projects, such as a rapid bus transit link in the Cape Town area, are currently under construction.

MEDIA AND COMMUNICATIONS

South Africa's media and communications systems are now the most modern in Africa. During apartheid, however, the media was censored. Criticism of the government was not permitted. Books, articles, films, or plays that presented apartheid in a negative way were banned. Radio, with few stations, was state controlled and strictly censored. TV was not broadcast nationally until 1976 —on one station—because the government did not want South Africans to see any multiracial programs from abroad. The government took great pains to isolate South Africa from the world so that extreme racial segregation would seem normal.

▼ A bulk cargo vessel takes on grain at Durban. Durban is South Africa's busiest port, with extensive docks lining the shore.

South Africa's new constitution guarantees the freedom of the press. Newspapers, TV, and other media are now regularly critical of the government. Indeed, suggestions of corruption published in the media have led to the downfall of several prominent politicians, including Winnie Madikizela-Mandela, the divorced wife of Nelson Mandela. The state-run South African Broadcasting Company (SABC) is the main broadcaster. The country also enjoys a TV subscription channel and numerous satellite channels. The SABC broadcasts on both TV and radio in English, Afrikaans, and many Bantu as well as other languages. More than 350 radio stations now operate. Of the many daily papers published in various languages, *The Sowetan* is the top seller in English.

Telecommunications are well developed within large cities, but much less developed in country areas. In 2002, South Africa had 4.8 million landline phones, with an estimated 16.8 million cellular phones in 2003. Cell phone use has risen steeply since 1997. In 2002, less than one-twelfth of the population had personal computers, and use of the Internet was also limited, with about

3.1 million users. In rural areas and townships, there is often little access to computers, the Internet, or any telephones. Centers such as Soweto Digital Village are being set up to ease these problems, and computer resource centers provide training in computer use.

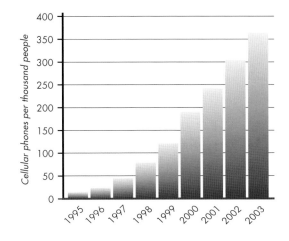

▲ Cellular phone use, 1995–2003

 Did You Know?

In 2005, South Africa ranked 26 out of 167 countries in terms of press freedom. This ranking put it ahead of the UK, Australia, and Japan.

◄ A customer at a Cape Town barber shop uses a cell phone. These phones have eased communication difficulties in some parts of South Africa, although network coverage remains patchy for many.

CHAPTER 10

Education and Health

In 2002, South Africa spent 8.7 percent of its Gross Domestic Product on health and 5.3 percent on education. The education percentage is one of the highest of any nation, and it looks ready to rise to more than 8 percent by 2008.

EDUCATION

During the apartheid era, South Africa's education system was strongly biased toward whites. Large sums were spent on the education of white children, while nonwhite schools had scant resources. Nonwhite parents struggled to meet the costs of tuition, uniforms, and books. Under apartheid, class sizes of 50 or more were common in black schools, while many white classes had about 20 pupils. Many nonwhites failed to complete their schooling, particularly during the period of uprising from 1976 to 1990.

Racism severely limited higher education. Although whites were a minority of South Africa's people, out of sixteen universities in the 1970s and 1980s, eleven were for whites only,

three for black students, and one each for Asians and people of mixed race. Not surprisingly, an early 1990s survey found that almost all white adults were literate, but only 85 percent of Asians, 75 percent of Coloureds, and 50 percent of blacks. Since 1994, the government has spent large sums tackling these problems, with good success. In 2003, 86 percent of South Africa's total population were literate.

The government now aims to provide ten years of education for all children, regardless of race, language, or gender. All schools charge fees, but low-income families qualify for fee exemptions. School is compulsory between the ages of seven and fifteen (grades 1 through 9). Children under seven may attend nursery school. Children attend primary school for grades 1 to 7, and move to high school for grades 8 to 9. After grade 9, children may continue with their education for another three years, to grade 12, but this is not compulsory. In the early 2000s, about 90 percent of all children enrolled at

◀ A math lesson in progress at a primary school in Cape Town. Class sizes in mainly black schools are becoming smaller, thanks to the government's commitment to provide equal educational opportunities for all.

primary school, but only about 50 percent of pupils completed their secondary education.

South Africa's twenty-one universities and fifteen *technikons*, or technical colleges, are open to all students with the required grades. More that 1 million students now attend higher education institutions every year. In 2004, South Africa began to reform its higher education system, with smaller institutions becoming parts of larger ones and technical

colleges redefined as universities. As well as education for young people, the government promotes adult education to address the lack of schooling among those whose education was restricted by apartheid laws and disrupted by the antiapartheid struggle. The government's Adult Basic Education and Training (ABET) program provides secondary-level schooling particularly for the so-called "lost generation" that missed out on school.

Education and Health

- Life expectancy at birth, male: 45
- Life expectancy at birth, female: 46.5
- Infant mortality rate per 1,000: 53
- Under five mortality rate per 1,000: 66
- Physicians per 1,000 people: 0.7
- Health expenditure as % of GDP: 8.7%
- Education expenditure as % of GDP: 5.3%
- Primary net enrollment: 90%
- Pupil-teacher ratio, primary school: 35.4
- Adult literacy as % age 15+: 86%

Source: United Nations Agencies and World Bank

Focus on: Language and Schooling

The language in which lessons are taught is a crucial issue in South Africa. In 1976, the government ruled that black students be taught in Afrikaans, then the language of apartheid, instead of English. This rule led to the uprising in Soweto, a major milestone in the struggle against apartheid. Primary students now learn in their own languages, but English and Afrikaans are still used at higher levels. Many people feel that African languages are being sidelined by the government's education policy, which fails to challenge English as the dominant tongue.

◀ South Africa's higher education institutions are now multiracial, as this scene in a dining hall at the University of the Western Cape shows. Courses are open to all students who earn the required grades.

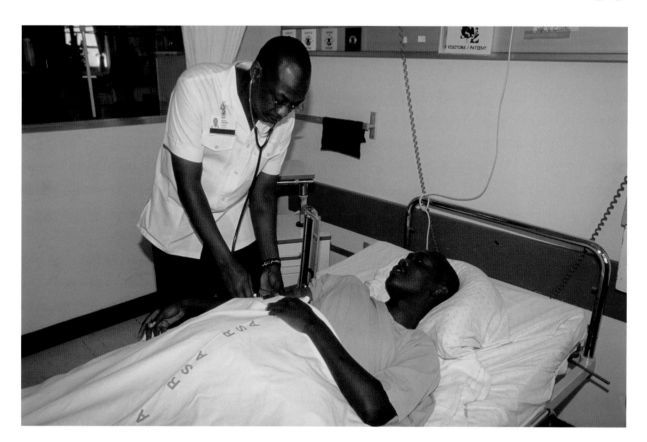

▲ A doctor examines a patient at the Groote Schuur Hospital in Cape Town, where the world's first heart transplant was performed. Such excellence in medical care is not enjoyed by all South Africans.

HEALTH

In the early 1990s, the average life expectancy for white people was ten years higher than that for blacks, Coloureds, and Asians. This gap was another legacy of apartheid, during which far more money was spent on medical facilities for whites than for everyone else. Whites who could afford to pay received excellent care, while in nonwhite settlements, medical centers were scarce and underfunded. In townships and rural areas, poor housing, malnutrition, and lack of clean water and sanitation caused diseases such as tuberculosis, cholera, malaria, and bilharzia (a worm infection spread through infected water) to be widespread.

In 1994, up to 12 million South Africans were without access to clean drinking water, with up to 20 million without proper sanitation, and 2.3 million malnourished. The ANC vowed to work toward providing all South Africans with equal access to medical care—a challenge of immense proportions. The government commissioned new hospitals and clinics and prioritized training of medical staff. It placed particular importance on ending malnutrition. Pregnant women and children were given free medical care. These policies have brought some improvements in health, but in 2004, there was still less than one doctor (0.7) for every 1,000 people (compared to 1.7 per 1,000 in the UK and 5.5 per 1,000 in the United States). In 2002, 5.9 million people remained without access to a safe source of drinking water, and 14.9 million people still did not have adequate sanitation.

At the start of the twenty-first century, a huge variety of medical practices coexist in South Africa. Along with orthodox medicine, South Africans can access faith healers, herbalists, and healers who practice divination (using natural signs to diagnose the cause of illness). Practitioners of all kinds are recognized by the new regime, and most are engaged in the effort to raise awareness of health issues.

Did You Know?

In 2004, 27.9 percent of pregnant women in South Africa were HIV-positive.

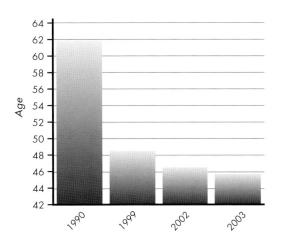

▲ Life expectancy at birth 1990–2003

Focus on: HIV/AIDS

Since 1994, a major health crisis has arisen—HIV/AIDS. In 2004, 21.5 percent of the adult population in South Africa had HIV/AIDS, and 5.3 million adults and children were infected with HIV—the highest figure of any country in the world. The ANC has been widely criticized for its slowness in reacting to the epidemic, at first failing to acknowledge the extent of the problem and to devote adequate funds to tackling it. As a result, HIV spread quickly. Large sums have now been committed to fight the disease. The high incidence of HIV/AIDS accounts for the steep fall in the average life expectancy in South Africa since 1990 (*see graph*). Studies in 2004 suggested that the infection rate may soon start to level off, with the number of deaths peaking in 2008.

◀ Demonstrators wear HIV-positive T-shirts to challenge prejudice about HIV/AIDS on a march in the Eastern Cape to mark World AIDS day.

CHAPTER 11

Culture and Religion

The ethnic mix of South Africa's "rainbow nation" has given rise to a rich and varied culture in terms of the arts, cuisine, and religious beliefs. The roots of black South African culture are thousands of years old. From the seventeenth century on, Europeans, Asians, and other groups arrived with their own styles and cultures, some of which blended with older traditions to create new forms.

ART AND LITERATURE

South Africa has a rich artistic heritage dating back to prehistoric times. The earliest artists were the San Bushmen, whose rock paintings and carvings can be seen at hundreds of sites today. Mural painting, mask and jewelry making, wood and stone carving, basket weaving and beadwork are among traditional crafts. Starting in the 1650s, Europeans, Asians, and other immigrants brought new styles of painting and sculpture. In the mid-twentieth century, township art became important. Artists such as George Pemba and Mslaba Dumile depicted the harsh realities of daily township life in their work. Since 1994, the free and more fair post-apartheid era has brought a new flowering of arts and crafts.

South Africa has a rich literary heritage in English, Afrikaans, and the Bantu languages. Until relatively recently, however, the black literary tradition was mainly oral. Fables, proverbs, and poetry including *izibongo*, praise

▼ A park ranger shows San Bushmen rock paintings to visitors in the Kruger National Park.

poems, were handed down by being recited aloud. Olive Schreiner's *Story of an African Farm* (1883) and Percy FitzPatrick's *Jock of the Bushveld* (1907) were early stories in English depicting Afrikaner life.

The antiapartheid movement gave rise to important literary works including novels, plays, and poetry, by both white and black writers. Novels such as Alan Paton's *Cry the Beloved Country* (1948) and André Brink's *A Dry White Season* (1979) were banned in South Africa because they challenged the apartheid establishment. Nevertheless, they helped to

draw the world's attention to the injustices of minority rule. J.M. Coetzee is the only novelist to have won the British Booker Prize twice, while Nadine Gordimer was awarded the Nobel Prize for Literature in 1991. The works of Wilbur Smith and Bessie Head and Nelson Mandela's autobiography, *Long Walk to Freedom* (1994), are international bestsellers.

 Did You Know?

Insect foods such as fried locusts and *mopani* worms are a traditional source of protein in South Africa.

Focus on: South African Cuisine

South African cuisine is a varied mix of cooking from different cultures. Dutch, German, Huguenot, Indian, Malay, and Chinese immigrants have all contributed distinctive flavors and cooking styles. For example, Cape Malay cuisine features mild meat curries flavored with spiced fruits. Indian cooking is hot and spicy. Most European dishes are meat or fish based. *Potjiekos*, a stew cooked in a three-legged pot, is a popular recipe. Dried meat, called by its Afrikaans name *biltong*, is chewy but nourishing. Perhaps the most characteristic form of cooking is the *braai,* or outdoor barbecue. Barbecued chops, kebabs, and *boerewor*s, or spicy sausages, are served with salads and washed down with local wine or beer. In contrast to these high-protein meals, the diet of many poorer Africans is very simple and low in protein. The staple food is maize, called mealie, made into a porridge called pap or used to make meat or vegetable stews.

◄ A craftswoman makes beadwork in a Cape Town workshop. Beadwork produced by projects such as this is sold internationally, including to large stores in London, New York, Paris, and Tokyo.

PERFORMING ARTS

Music and dance have always been central to
celebrations in South Africa, as well as being
part of everyday life. An amazing range of
musical styles can be heard, from classical to
Cape Malay, jazz, soul, reggae, and pop. Black,
Asian, and Coloured musicians bring their own
distinctive sounds to western styles from rock to
rap. *Kwela* music features the plaintive sound of
the penny whistle. *Kwaito* is a fairly new style
from the townships, influenced by *toyi-toyi*—
protest chants.

During the apartheid years, jazz musicians such
as Abdullah Ibrahim, Hugh Masekela, Miriam
Makeba, and Jonas Gwangwa left South Africa
to become internationally famous. Makeba was
exiled from South Africa in 1960 because of her
appearance in the antiapartheid movie *Come
Back Africa*. Both Makeba and Masekela sang,
among other things, about the hardships of
apartheid and the need to overthrow it. In the
post-apartheid era, many musicians have
returned home. South Africa has a rich choral
tradition including gospel music and Zulu
mbube (unaccompanied choir singing).
Ladysmith Black Mambazo, which joined
forces for a time with U.S. singer-songwriter
Paul Simon, is one of the best-known groups.

RELIGION

South Africa's diverse people follow many
different faiths. More than 8 percent follow
traditional African religions, which recognize
the influence of ancestral spirits. Spirit
mediums called *sangoma* make the connection
between ordinary people and the spirit world.

▼ A group of *a capella*, or unaccompanied,
singers produces multipart harmonies to
entertain visitors at the Victoria and Alfred
Waterfront in Cape Town.

More than 80 percent of South Africans are Christians of different denominations. Most Afrikaans-speakers belong to the Dutch Reformed Church. English-speakers include Anglicans, Roman Catholics, Presbyterians, and Methodists. Christianity gained hold among black communities in the early 1800s, as black Africans fled the advance of powerful Zulu armies under the Zulu chief Shaka during a

series of wars called the *mfecane,* or "crushing." Thousands of black Africans sought refuge in Christian missions and were subsequently converted. African independent churches such as the Zion Christian Church blend Christian and traditional beliefs. Significant numbers of Muslims and Hindus also practice their faiths in South Africa. Each religion has its own festivals. Christian festivals such as Christmas and Good Friday are public holidays, along with days that celebrate South African history, such as Freedom Day, which commemorates the first democratic election on April 27, 1994.

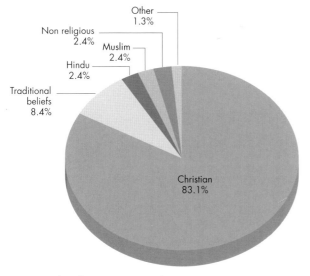

▲ South Africa's major religions

? Did You Know?

South Africa's public holidays include Human Rights Day (March 21), the Day of Reconciliation (December 16) and the Day of Goodwill (December 26).

▼ Members of the Church of Zion, which has a mainly Zulu congregation, conduct a baptism in the sea near Durban.

CHAPTER 12

Leisure and Tourism

In the early 2000s, differences in income and living standards among South Africans still affected leisure patterns. The majority had lived in poverty and enjoyed little opportunity for leisure, working long hours to feed their families and taking little time off. During the apartheid years, the migrant labor system split families for months, often years. Men had to work in distant industries with little leisure time or chance to see their families. Whites-only cities and suburbs were well-supplied with facilities such as parks, sports and community centers, swimming pools, cinemas, cafés, bars, and clubs, while in townships and rural areas, these facilities were sparse or nonexistent.

Since 1994, the government has worked to improve leisure facilities for blacks, Coloureds, and Asians, both in cities and in the vast countryside. Increased prosperity among some of these groups has meant that more people are able to take time off and get away at least once a year, whether to meet up with distant relatives, go to a beach or national park, or see more of their country. In 2002, nearly 3.8 million South Africans took vacations abroad.

South Africa's sunny climate allows people to spend a lot of free time outdoors. All over the country, children gather on open ground to play soccer, cricket, traditional ball games, or tag, known as *kho-kho*. Board games such as

▼ Boys play soccer in Cape Town. Soccer is one of the sports enjoyed by all South Africans—regardless of color.

checkers or the traditional game of *morabaraba*, played with tokens called "cows," are very popular. Elaborate toys such as model cars are made from odds and ends, such as wire. South Africans are also enthusiastic TV viewers and moviegoers, with TVs and radios treasured possessions in many households. Township-dwellers who do not possess these items may catch the latest gossip or a TV program at a local bar, called a *shebeen*.

SPORTS

South Africa has a proud sporting tradition, but for much of the twentieth century, white people had far better sports facilities than everyone else. Nonwhites were usually excluded from playing in national teams. As criticism of apartheid grew abroad, South African teams were barred from international competitions, including the Olympic Games.

The ban was lifted in the early 1990s. The South African Sports Commission is working to improve sports facilities and opportunities for everyone. Traditional games and sports, such as stick-fighting—with two sticks, one to strike and the other to parry— and *dibeke*, a ball game, are actively encouraged.

Soccer is the most popular sport among all sections of the community. More than 15,000 clubs compete at various levels, and the country has a huge following for national and major league teams. Rugby Union is also popular, especially among Afrikaners. Joy rocked the country in 1995, when South Africa hosted and

▼ Swimmers from the South African 4 x 100 meter freestyle relay team celebrate victory at the 2004 Olympic Games in Athens. Swimming is among the sports still dominated by whites in South Africa.

won the Rugby World Cup. Whites still dominate rugby at the national level, despite efforts to promote the game among blacks, Coloureds, and Asians. Cricket, boxing, netball, athletics, tennis, and horseracing are also popular. Golf has produced some well-known names, such as Gary Player and Ernie Els. Many people keep fit by cycling, jogging, or swimming. The Comrades Marathon (54 miles/87.6 km between Durban and Pietermaritzburg) and the Two Oceans Marathon (35 miles/56 km on the Cape peninsula) are two long, gruelling, South African super-marathons.

TOURISM

The tourist industry has grown rapidly since apartheid ended. In 1986, just 300,000 tourists visited South Africa. Tourist figures increased dramatically after democratization, and have continued to climb steadily, to 6.5 million in 2003 —a tenfold increase in ten years. Because tourism is a major source of foreign income, the government promotes the industry, for example regulating and rating accommodations and supporting township tours. About 10 percent of the workforce is employed within the tourist industry, whether running hotels, shops, or restaurants, working as guides, wardens, or drivers, or making handicrafts for souvenirs.

South Africa's spectacular scenery and wildlife are major attractions. Tourists may drive the "garden route," a scenic stretch of coastline between Cape Town and Port Elizabeth, view the unique fynbos vegetation of the Western Cape, head for the beaches around Durban, or hike, bike, or climb in the Drakensberg.

▼ During the apartheid era, political prisoners, including Nelson Mandela, were held on Robben Island off Cape Town. The island is now a popular tourist attraction. Here, a guide who was himself once a prisoner shows visitors around.

National parks such as the Kruger are major draws. Visitors may take a safari-style vacation, go bungee jumping or white-water rafting, or explore the traditional cultures of peoples such as the Zulu and Ndebele. The townships have tapped into the tourist trade, with township tours providing income for poor communities. Security can be an issue for tourists, however, with high rates of both car theft and mugging.

 Did You Know?

Robben Island off Cape Town, where Nelson Mandela spent much of his imprisonment, is now a UNESCO World Heritage Site.

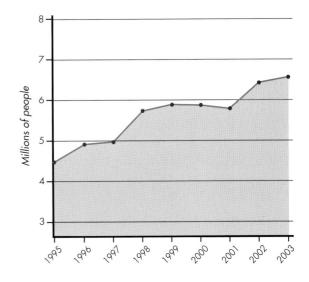

▲ Changes in international tourism, 1995–2003

Tourism in South Africa

- Tourist arrivals, millions: 6.505
- Earnings from tourism in U.S. $: 5,232,000,000
- Tourism as % foreign earnings: 11.5%
- Tourist departures, millions: 3.794
- Expenditure on tourism in U.S. $: 3,232,000,000

Source: World Bank

Focus on: Kruger National Park

On the border with Mozambique, the Kruger National Park is South Africa's largest national park. Covering 7,580 sq miles (19,633 sq km), an area the size of Israel, the reserve dates back to 1898. Visitors may stay in a variety of shelters, including tents, lodges, and *rondavels* (thatched round houses). People drive or take a safari bus to view zebras, giraffes, antelope and the "big five:" lion, rhino, leopard, elephant, and buffalo.

▲ Tourists in the Kruger National Park travel in vehicles like this to view potentially dangerous wildlife, such as these rhinoceroses, in safety.

CHAPTER 13

Environment and Conservation

South Africa's wildlife and vegetation are among the most diverse of any nation. Protection of the natural world lies in the care of the government's Ministry of Environmental Affairs, which has taken a leading role since 1994. The new constitution guarantees the "environmental rights" of all citizens—the right to a healthy environment, both now and for future generations. The government claims significant success in conserving energy,

▼ In August 2000, environmentalists launched a major conservation effort to clean and move jackass penguins away from an oil slick that threatened their breeding grounds on Dassen Island, near Cape Town.

preventing erosion, and reducing air, marine, and noise pollution. Environmental needs sometimes conflict with government pledges, for example, the promise to improve the standard of housing and the provision of water and sanitation to townships and shanty towns and to some rural areas.

POLLUTION AND WASTE MANAGEMENT

Mining, industry, agriculture, and growing cities all cause problems for the environment. Mining practices pollute the land, with giant waste heaps littering the skyline around cities such as Johannesburg. Dredging for diamonds

▲ A pall of smog hangs in the air over Cape Town. Many South African cities are plagued by this poisonous haze.

and other minerals also harms marine and wetland environments. Recently, the government has halted plans to mine the dunes on the shores of Lake St. Lucia near Richards Bay because of the environmental damage that would have resulted. In this instance, jobs that may be lost due to the prevention of mining could be compensated for by the expansion in tourism around the lake. Mining and overgrazing by livestock also cause erosion and desertification, or growing "dustbowl" areas. Similar problems can arise when forests are felled or natural grasslands are plowed up.

Many of South Africa's rivers, wetlands, and coastal waters are polluted in varying degrees by pesticides and fertilizers from agriculture. Lack of water is a general problem because of frequent droughts, and water sources are also being depleted by increasing demands from farms, factories, and cities. The government's water conservation agency has launched a major campaign, "Working for Water," to preserve scant supplies—for example, by clearing nonnative plants and trees from water courses and catchment areas. Accidental spills

of toxic chemicals, such as oil, periodically pollute coastal waters, endangering marine life. Such spills involve expensive clean-up operations. South Africa has signed several international treaties that restrict dumping waste at sea, including the Law of the Sea and the Ship Pollution treaty.

Air pollution is a problem, especially in industrial and urban areas. Waste gases from factories and car exhausts create health concerns, such as breathing problems. Sulphur dioxide and nitrogen oxide from cars, power stations, and factories give rise to acid rain, which harms land and wetland life. South Africa has signed several treaties to protect air quality, including the Climate Change, Kyoto Protocol, and Ozone Protection treaties. The ANC actively encourages the reuse of resources, such as timber, and the recycling of glass, metal, paper, and other materials to curb pollution and also reduce the problem of waste disposal.

CONSERVATION EFFORTS

South Africa's wildlife includes many plants and animals found nowhere else. An amazing 80 percent of its plants, 30 percent of its reptiles, 15 percent of its mammals, and 6 percent of its breeding birds are unique. Before the arrival of Europeans, vast herds of grazers, such as springbok, wildebeest, and zebra, roamed the veld. During the eighteenth and early nineteenth centuries, white hunters decimated these herds for meat, sport, and to clear the land for domestic stock. The once-prolific bluebuck, the Cape lion, and the quagga, a subspecies of zebra, were all hunted to extinction.

Fortunately, the conservation movement became active fairly early, with organizations such as the Wildlife and Environmental Society of South Africa, which was founded in 1926. Campaign groups put pressure on governments to set aside wilderness areas. The conservation movement gathered pace in the 1930s. Hunting is now confined to private game reserves where animals are specifically raised for this purpose.

Habitat loss poses a serious threat to wildlife. Expanding cities, industrial areas, and farms encroach on wild areas. For example, on the Cape Flats outside Cape Town, sprawling suburbs, factory land, and small farms have swallowed up huge tracts of wild grassland and wetland. The government has pledged to protect the nation's wildlife and scenic beauty both for their own sake and to safeguard the lucrative tourist industry. South Africa now has more than 500 protected sites including 20 national parks and numerous reserves, marine sanctuaries, and botanical

Focus on: Biodiversity

South Africa has been called the "greatest wildlife show on earth." Among its 247 species are the world's largest land animal, the African elephant; the fastest mammal, the cheetah; and the tallest animal, the giraffe. More than 300 species of breeding birds include colorful bee-eaters and two flightless birds: the jackass penguin and the ostrich, the world's largest bird. Reptiles include crocodiles, sea turtles, and snakes, some of which are highly poisonous.

► South African game reserves are regularly patrolled by wardens to protect wildlife such as rhinos and elephants from poachers, who would kill the animals for their horns and tusks.

gardens. Several new national parks have been designated since 1994, including Table Mountain. In 2003, 6.2 percent of the nation's land area was protected. While representing a huge area, this figure falls short of the 10 percent recommended for all countries by the International Union for the Conservation of Nature (IUCN).

? Did You Know?

South Africa's national parks have scored some notable successes in preserving rare species. Kruger National Park's population of elephants rose from 7,468 to 8,371 in the six years between 1989 and 1995. Its white rhino population rose from 1,284 to 2,800 during the same time.

Environmental and Conservation Data

🗁 Forested area as % total land area: 4%

🗁 Protected area as % total land area: 6.2%

🗁 Number of protected areas: 528

SPECIES DIVERSITY

Category	Known species	Threatened species
Mammals	247	42
Breeding birds	304	28
Reptiles	364	19
Amphibians	117	9
Fish	629	29
Plants	23,420	45

Source: World Resources Institute

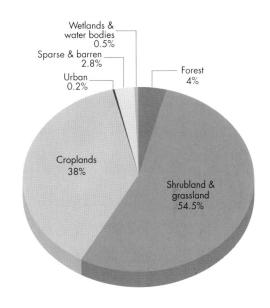

Wetlands & water bodies 0.5%
Sparse & barren 2.8%
Urban 0.2%
Forest 4%
Croplands 38%
Shrubland & grassland 54.5%

▲ Types of habitat as a percentage of total area.

◄ A humpback whale surfaces off the South African coast. Some 2,000 of these marine mammals pass along the coast as they shuttle between their antarctic feeding grounds and the warm waters off Mozambique, where they breed.

CHAPTER 14

Future Challenges

The last thirty years have seen a radical transformation in South Africa. Against all the odds, the country has achieved a relatively peaceful transition from apartheid to democracy. The dramatic events of the 1990s, however, did not close the gap in living standards between whites and blacks, Coloureds, and Asians that was the legacy of apartheid. After the sky-high hopes of the early 1990s, some people inevitably became disillusioned about the rate of progress and the government's delivery of its promises.

LIFE AFTER APARTHEID

The 1994 government was elected on an immensely ambitious program. It pledged to provide jobs and improve life for millions of less-privileged citizens, while bringing about reconciliation between races. Much damage had to be undone. In the early 2000s, the ANC pursued a cautious but effective economic policy, controlling inflation and creating jobs by encouraging free trade and private investment. The period saw some economic growth, but not enough to reduce unemployment significantly, despite the many thousands of jobs created by the Reconstruction and Development Programme and other employment initiatives.

Law and order remain a problem. Relaxation of border controls after 1994 has allowed international criminal organizations to gain

▼ United Nations peacekeepers from South Africa point out a hill that forms a buffer zone between rival army factions fighting in the hills near Kilalo, eastern Congo. The fighting forced thousands to flee. In December 2004, the South African troops helped to secure the buffer zone between the rival groups, but the area remains dangerous.

a foothold in South Africa. The country has become a major center for drug trafficking. The incidence of violent crime remains very high, causing many wealthy citizens to move from city centers to gated suburbs that provide more security. Starting in the mid-1990s, HIV/AIDS caused a major health crisis, which many believe the government only started to handle effectively in the early 2000s.

HOPES FOR THE FUTURE

Despite these problems, South Africa's economic future looks fairly bright. In the foreseeable future, the country looks ready to continue as Africa's leading economy. Its

 Did You Know?

In the early 2000s, half of all government spending went to social services, including health and education, yet many areas still lack adequate hospitals and schools.

strengths include its large mineral reserves such as gold, diamonds, and platinum, and also coal to fuel growing industries. South Africa's well-developed infrastructure will continue to be an important asset on a continent where essential infrastructure is often missing. After more than a decade of liberal, stable government, South Africa will continue to play a major role in both African politics and international affairs.

Since 1994, the government has made considerable progress in empowering disadvantaged sectors of the community. In just more than ten years, a new black middle class has arisen, but millions, mostly black, still live in poverty. The gulf between the haves and have-nots is still huge, posing a major obstacle to peace and security. After conquering apartheid and giving all races the right to vote, the people of South Africa have made progress in the immense task of equalizing wealth, power, and influence in South Africa, but much remains to be done.

▼ A group of boys and girls enjoy friendship in Khayelitsha, Cape Town's biggest township. South Africans have cause to be optimistic about the future, although many challenges remain from the apartheid era.

Time Line

ca. 8,000 B.C. San Bushmen and Khoekhoen roam South Africa.

ca. A.D. 100 Bantu-speaking Nguni groups move into South Africa.

ca. 1300s and 1400s Sotho, Tswana, Tonga, and Venda move into South Africa.

1652 Dutch East India Company founds a settlement at Cape Town.

1806 British take over Cape Colony from the Dutch.

1820–1830 Zulus under King Shaka extend their territory, causing other African peoples to flee.

1836–1854 In the Great Trek, 16,000 Boers migrate north from the Cape to escape British rule. Dutch Boers found two republics, the Transvaal and Orange Free State.

1840s–1906 British and Boer armies defeat African chiefdoms and take over their lands.

1843 Natal becomes a British colony.

1867 Diamonds are discovered near Kimberley.

1880–1881 Boers defeat the British in the First Boer War.

1886 Gold is discovered in the Witwatersrand at what is now Johannesburg.

1899–1902 The Second Boer War ends with a British victory.

1906 The last armed black rebellion, the Bambatha Rebellion, is suppressed.

1910 British colonies of Natal and the Cape and the two Boer republics are united in the Union of South Africa.

1912 The African National Congress (ANC) is founded.

1913 Natives' Land Act reserves all but 13 percent of South Africa for the minority white population and makes it illegal for blacks, the majority population, to own land.

1923 Native Urban Areas Act restricts blacks to separate areas in cities.

1948 The National Party wins power in South Africa and sets up the apartheid system.

1950 The Population Registration Act classifies South Africans into groups: blacks, whites, Asians, and Coloureds.

1952 Pass Laws require nonwhites to carry identity papers.

1960 South African police commit the Sharpeville Massacre. The ANC and allied groups are banned.

1961 *Umkhonto we Sizwe* (MK, the Spear of the Nation) begins its armed struggle. South Africa becomes a republic and is expelled from the British Commonwealth.

1964 Nelson Mandela is sentenced to life imprisonment.

1960s–1970s Bantustan Acts create ten *bantustans* (homelands) in poor areas for black Africans.

1974 South Africa is expelled from the United Nations.

1976 Soweto Uprising is begun by Sowetan schoolchildren who protest having their classes taught in Afrikaans.

1983 The National Party declares a state of emergency.

1986 The United States, EEC, and Commonwealth impose trade sanctions on South Africa to protest apartheid.

1988 The South African army invades Angola but it is defeated.

1989 National Party candidate F. W. de Klerk is elected president of South Africa and desegrates many facilities.

1990 ANC is unbanned and Nelson Mandela is released.

1991 Apartheid laws are scrapped.

1994 South Africa holds its first democratic election, with victory for the ANC. Nelson Mandela is elected president. The Reconstruction and Development Programme is launched to help heal the wounds of apartheid.

1996–1998 The Truth and Reconciliation Commission, chaired by Archbishop Desmond Tutdu, conducts hearings about abuses and crimes under apartheid.

1999 ANC wins a second election victory. Nelson Mandela steps down as president and Thabo Mbeki replaces him.

2003 Government approves major program to tackle HIV/AIDS.

2004 ANC wins a third election victory.

2005 Vice-president Jacob Zuma leaves office.

2006 Congress of South African Trade Unions (COSATU) calls for a strike to protest the stalemate at the World Trade Organization trade talks in Switzerland.

Glossary

acid rain rain that is slightly acidic because it is polluted by waste gases from car exhausts and power stations

Afrikaner a white South African of mainly Dutch descent

amnesty a general pardon

apartheid the South African government's policy of separate development and strict segregation for people of different races, in force between the 1950s and the early 1990s

bantustan a term meaning "homelands for Bantus" describing the areas set aside for black Africans to live in during the apartheid era

Boer another word for an Afrikaner, the term *boer* means "farmer" in Afrikaans

British Commonwealth an organization made up of countries that once formed part of the British Empire

Coloured the term used in South Africa for people of mixed race, which also includes groups such as the Cape Malays and Khoisans

compensation an award, usually of money, paid to someone to make up for a wrong that has been done

constitution a set of rules governing a country or an organization

cyclone a revolving tropical storm, also known as a hurricane

democracy a political system in which members of the government are chosen by adults voting in free elections

denomination a branch of a particular religion

epidemic a major outbreak of disease

erosion the wearing away of the land by natural forces such as wind, rain, and ice, sometimes increased by deforestation or overgrazing by animals

ethnic classification of people according to their racial, cultural, religious, tribal, national, or linguistic origins

fossil fuel coal, oil, gas, and other fuels formed of fossilized remains of plants or animals that lived millions of years ago

fynbos the unique vegetation and biome of the Southwestern Cape region of South Africa, which includes plants such as irises, pelargoniums and proteas; the word means "fine-leaved bush" in Afrikaans

Gross Domestic Product (GDP) the total value of the goods and services produced by a country in a year

Huguenots French Protestants who emigrated to South Africa and other places to escape persecution in Catholic France in the late seventeenth century

human rights rights, including economic, social, and political rights, possessed by all people simply because they are human and deserve to be treated with respect

indentured worker a laborer who is bound for a time to work, usually for the price of travel, food, and lodging

industrialization the process of developing a country's industries and manufacturing

inflation a general increase in prices within a country

informal economy the sector of the economy in which employment is unofficial, so that employers can avoid government regulations and employees avoid paying taxes

infrastructure the facilities needed for a country to function, including communications and transportation

judicial relating to the courts and justice

legislative relating to laws and law-making

literacy the ability to read and write

mineral one of the naturally occurring, nonliving substances of which rocks are made

plankton the tiny plants and animals that float on the surface of the oceans and form the base of marine food chains that feed larger animals of all kinds

plateau a flat-topped area of high ground

proportional representation a system of electing members of parliament by giving seats to political parties according to their share of the vote in the whole country

race a class of people who share a common genetic origin

regime a government in power for certain period of time

republic a state or form of government without a monarch

sanctions bans, usually on trading, also known as boycotts; sanctions are used to withhold support and to put economic pressure on nations or organizations in an attempt to get them to change their policies or practices

sanitation the provision of sewerage to carry away waste and also standards of public hygiene generally

segregation the practice of separating people according to race, gender, age, or some other criterion

squatter camps illegal shanty towns, usually occurring on the edges of cities without permission from the authorities

subsistence farming a type of agriculture in which farmers grow food for their own needs, with little left over to sell for profit

tornado a whirlwind, which is a revolving column of air

townships the name given to urban areas that grew up in South Africa on the outskirts of cities or industrial areas before and during the apartheid era, created to house the black workers who staffed the mines, factories, or service industries; unlike squatter camps, these settlements were permitted by the authorities and, in many cases, were mandated housing areas for nonwhites

Further Information

BOOKS TO READ

Bowden, Rob, and Tony Binns.
Changing Face of South Africa.
Hodder Wayland, 2004.

Brett, Michael.
South Africa. DK Eyewitness
Travel Guides (series).
Dorling Kindersley, 2003.

Downing, David.
Nelson Mandela. Leading Lives (series).
Heinemann Library, 2004.

Graham, Ian.
South Africa. Country File (series).
Franklin Watts, 2004.

Green, Jen.
South Africa. Nations of the World (series).
Raintree Publishers, 2000.

Mandela, Nelson.
Long Walk to Freedom.
Time Warner Books, 2000.

Mitchell, Jason.
South Africa. Insight Guide (series).
Insight Guides, 2003.

Roberts, Martin.
*South Africa 1948-1994 the Rise and Fall of
Apartheid (Longman History Project).*
Longman, 2001.

USEFUL WEB SITES

African Studies Center, University of Pennsylvania
www.africa.upenn.edu/Country_Specific/
S_Africa.html

BBC news country profile on South Africa
news.bbc.co.uk/1/hi/world/africa/country_profil
es/1071886.stm

*CIA World Factbook, providing current statistics
on South Africa*
www.cia.gov/cia/publications/factbook/geos/
sf.html

*Information about South Africa's geography,
economy, government, and people*
www.infoplease.com/ipa/A0107983.html

*South Africa Tourist Board's official site, with
national parks and other tourist attractions*
www.southafrica.net/

The South African government site
www.gov.za/

Publisher's note to educators and parents: Our editors
have carefully reviewed these Web sites to ensure that
they are suitable for children. Many Web sites change
frequently, however, and we cannot guarantee that a
site's future contents will continue to meet our high
standards of quality and educational value. Be advised
that children should be closely supervised whenever
they access the Internet.

Index

Page numbers in **bold** indicate pictures.

About the Author

Dr. Jen Green received a doctorate from the University of Sussex (Department of English and American Studies) in 1982. She worked in publishing for fifteen years and is now a full-time writer who has written more than 150 books for children. She lives in Great Britain.